COMPANION GRASSES

COMPANION GRASSES
BRIAN TEARE

OMNIDAWN PUBLISHING
RICHMOND, CALIFORNIA
2013

Cover Art:
Ives, Charles. Piano Sonata No. 2, "*Concord, Mass., 1840-60.*"
New York: Knickerbocker Press, 1921.
&
· Photographs taken by Brian Teare at Chimney Rock,
Point Reyes National Seashore, July 2012.

Book cover and interior design by Cassandra Smith

Cataloguing-in-Publication Data is available from the Library of Congress.

Published by Omnidawn Publishing, Richmond, California
www.omnidawn.com   (510) 237-5472   (800) 792-4957
10 9 8 7 6 5 4 3 2
ISBN: 978-1-890650-79-7

for Robert Barber

&

Jane Mead

&

in memory of

Robert J. Teare
(1933-2007)

Reginald Shepherd
(1963-2008)

Robin Blaser
(1925-2009)

> ...and the sacred,
> after I thought it was beauty, takes
> place constantly, ends constantly,
> to begin constantly, such violence,
> such sacred chance, so "you" whom
> I loved would find the crystal
> without difference, would form
> and reform   the perfection, the
> option   and come back

—Robin Blaser

Contents

III

I

WHITE GRAPHITE

(Limantour Beach)

the spit's edge open
to ocean goes pure

contour : in absence
of light, self's how

a tern's clutch nests
in next to nothing :

beach without moon
mere rumor, blur's

texture a scumble
scoured of color :

watery dense deep
stipple above sand

after rain, sky trues
its blues, the real

a profusion : seaweed
reek, the pink shatter

of crabshells, lupine
fat in dune grass,

surf sounding long
before I smell salt :

matter a mere shift
in limits, even skin's

a trick of the liminal :
touch here & I give

way to elsewhere :

SUSURRUS STANZAS
(*Sutro Baths*)

"Sound is sea: pattern lapping pattern."—Ronald Johnson

/

pure ruin   a stanza open

to weather   the pool's rim

still tinted   an "aquatic" blue

stanza   as in stance   as in

a way of standing   the way of

wild iris   their smaller yellow

petal threads   slight as saffron

the *there*   where scale outpaces

the eye   lichen a line to horizon

stem to tide   a dilation

in which seeing   is thinking

to find a way   a language

to where   the human fails

/

the problem of presence of

incursion   of how far too

far is   ruin to ruinous   if

"human nature"   is "to stand

in the middle of a thing"

what is a nature   where

to stand   I want   to get

closer to where   material

touches language   "impatient

with ruins"   its obviate

architecture   its structure

lung   grammar   sung

mortar   undoing & undone

/

to write sight   is itself

site's re-vision   a visitor's

signature   as plastic is

among stones   busted

pipes rusting   gulls'

flight   pattern a graft

to updraft   they wheel

& land   wheedle trash

verbs urge the world's

semblance   into being

& dissemble   if

to stand *there*   is only

misprision   what is

this need to lead to ruin

/

it's beautiful   isn't it

this used-up   "seascape"

& isn't it also terror   isn't

it *a priori*   "essentially

mortuary"   to stand

at an edge   entirely

contingency   so far west

imagination ends

each day   in pre-fab

ruin   America

this place that outlives

its own demise

/

but coast   isn't

finished yet   with

the how-to-touch-it

tide turns waves

to noise   shivers

fizzing   spindrift

gifted wind sifts

to bricks   crashed

crests ended   there's

nothing but rhythm

to hit   vision

with image   until

the sentence breaks

to let in   the *there*

/

to open   farther

ocean   spit's edge

more sound   than

matter   & mind

no purchase   rock

where foot stands

flood   a wreck

of perspective

a site   to disappear

geological   time

where eye   turns ear

against will   to hear

& fills

/

& wants   two grammars

one affable to ocean   another

equal   to its sheet of silver

surface shook by light   & lifted

from blue rudiment   one pattern

translucent at noon   another

as crest to trough   verb's arc

from subject to dark   scintillant

predicate   "the sea's hostility

to memory   its passion

for erasure"   wed to sun sets

a pivot between joy & terror

it is true   it takes   one

sentence   two grammars to

marry the mutable to fundament

/

aseity   assay or *essay*

to be a beautiful word

above all   & wonder

just so   toward "world

& flesh   not as fact

or sum of facts   but

as locus of an inscription

of truth"   what I am

saying   a sight

to stand on   softly

fog enters   the stanza

open to weather

LITTLE ERRAND

I gather the rain

in both noun
& verb. The way

the river banks
its flood, floods
its banks, quiver's

grammar I carry

noiseless, easy
over my shoulder.

To aim is—I think
of his mouth.
Wet ripe apple's

scent : sugar,

leather. To aim
is a shaft tipped

with adamant. Angle,
grasp, aim is a way
to hope to take

what's struck in hand,

mouth. At the river
flood so lately laid

down damage by,
geese sleep, heads
turned under wings

wind tests tremor
in like archery's
physics shifts

energy, potential
to kinetic : flight—

but not yet :

this grammar's time
to string a bow, draw
taut the air, send rain

from quiver to verb
to aim to pierce

the scent of such red

flesh. Hope's arrow's
anatomy : thin,
feather's fletching

trembling, it
crests to end

in brightness.

QUAKINGGRASS
(*Briza Maxima*)

I've cut from summer—

    as if a swatch were possible—

    not collage exactly—

Gnats hovered above dirt

    path between chaparral

    (pretty word—Spanish—"evergreen oak")—

I envy the photo its frame—

    what I meant to say—

    to walk through gnats

Curtained between trees

    smelled "skunky"

    (his word)—

I followed him—

    no one had said "love" yet—

    high bluff cliffing the Pacific—

Spine of shadow

    we walked—

    temperate in the sense

Air felt without temperature—

    "riparian" gleaned from signage

    (prettier even—*rīpa*—"bank")—

Because the near river entered ocean

    I've cut from it—

    the way the photographer knows what lies

Beyond the frame—

    context is terrible weight—

    to describe the water's texture of

Gestures would never end—

    an inch of surface

    surfeit sense ("a detail overwhelms

Entirety," writes Barthes)—

    his storied thigh

    scarred just so

(Coin-sized pock marking

    loin)

    & tilted toward me—

Each image cropped but the frame—

    a lifetime—

    a coastline—

What is meant by context : to pose

    ruins the shot with intention—

    eye the I, he the camera—

Big Sur River a lagoon where it enters ocean—

    & there a willow grove—

    we waded out, we saw tide

Lift river & slip in—

    eddies edging the upriver bend—

    the privacy of being entered is

What I felt privy to—

    salt driving tide under- & upriver both—

    it came to us as counter-current—

Water swelled within itself—

    more forceful than the river

    entering itself

was pressure against my skin—

    as when I held his cock & his body

    bodied forth there—

Tender force

    rivering—

    his need to enter me—

An image pierced by the ear—

    a raptor over

    coastal fields—

Santa Lucia Mountains behind us—

    what is "lyric"—

    hawk, we thought—

(*Raptus* from *rapere*, "seize" or "rape")—

    its passing shadow triggered

    chill as it touched us—

Crow-sized, a harsh loud scream—

    the little book fell open, broken-spined—

    Sharp-shinned
    Cooper's
    Red-shouldered
    Broad-winged
    Swainson's
    Zone-tailed
    Red-tailed
    Rough-legged
    Ferruginous—

I imagined its passage over the field

    a ring of blackened grass—

    rust-colored tail broad, fanned, tipped with white—

A "sting, speck, cut" or "little hole" in the image—

    the attention taxonomy requires

    amounts to a species of singing—

A dark leading inner edge on the underwing—

    what is "lyric"—

    "subversive when *pensive*, when it thinks"—

(What he meant by frame)—

    the image came to him as the desire to have

    photographed the "right" thing—

He the I, eye the camera—

    what we saw as "beauty" meant only

    evening—

Swallows looped & dived to drink—

    "I should dump your sorry ass in the water," he said—

    to relate that which is spoken of

To the spatial & temporal context of the utterance—

    "Why do I always hold back?"—

    without it the image can't live—

A list of possible swallows—

    Tree, Bank, Cliff, Barn, Violet-green, Rough-winged—

    the migratory flyway's dwindling returns—

Without a frame the image

    a lens of air—

    the affair & the photograph

Sharing formal constraints—

    time, chance, light

    object

Invitation—

    the camera's aperture opened—

    neither of us would say, had said it—

Kept trying to stop meaning

    from taking final shape—

    a series, a story,

a pillow thrown against a mirror—

    one vista after another

    marked by signage : fence, bench—

By foot, by car, on credit, cash—

    socks impossibly burred—

    his sweaty black cap—

I gathered the grass from his hand—

    how "panicle" trembles

    (*panus*, "thread wound on a bobbin")—

Sweetly its crown to my face—

    (*pēnos*, "web")—

    pedicel, spikelet, glume & lemma—

Little grammar of attraction—

    inflorescence—

    (What is "lyric")—

The book fell open on its broken spine

    (*florere*, "to flower")—

    "It's quakinggrass," I said—

                         [*Big Sur, June 2006*]

LARGO

Now the rain

Now the seams   put in evening

Now the tree   seeming shakes out
of felt   unfolds cleanly

If in falling   rain names what it touches

If beneath the tree   a dry radius describes
form   steps forward   wearing its suit   of summer's dust

A quietus

My ear on your chest   where rest hems breath with thread
until   being is everywhere   an edge   a cloth's

periphery pinned with rocks   & we under

look up   dry out the light   turn
sleep to costume   Now the sleeves

Now clean buttons   to shut our eyes

Now our each seam gleams

TALL FLATSEDGE NOTEBOOK

(*Cyperus Eragrostis*)

[Chimney Rock,
Point Reyes
National Seashore]

A mile's hike outside the fence-enclosed vista point
we sat hillside so inside experience I wrote the wrong date
down—March twenty-second—noticing no thought
but things : "when I think they animate my interior speech,   [*The Visible*
they haunt it as the *little phrase*." Ocean-tilted, the whole   *and the Invisible*—
thing leaning green, coastal prairie poised pre-Spring   Maurice
a prosody for seeing landscape as aural, ambient trick   Merleau-Ponty]
to hear the ear's eye : far bass, near treble, I saw

I heard
low drone wind
cut by distant cliffs' sheer fall

Above it   below the hill

surf's purr

& nearer

wind-shirred grasses
bright brown birdsong

in back of one bee   far
barking seals—

there was this sense of good work done, whole
earth's curve panorama : a gray whale, migratory
Pacific. Sense of almost spring, flowering grasses
dead, almost done leaving, it was there, nearer me
than you : winter-weathered stemmy thing ending
black asterisks : seeds, sheaths, not much to see,
I wanted a name for it—why?

[*The Way of Love*—
   Luce Irigaray]

"The aim of thought

                        corresponds
to the building of a bridge—

practicable & mobile
between two subjects."

I wanted a *hello* sort of like *I know you* as if
to call a grass a subject like I can't back home :
urbanity : a class-based lack of grasses shared
by people, fog, sidewalks, architecture, money,
the smells of jasmine & feces, & five sounds :

[59 Albion St.
San Francisco]

suck of tread in water

window clicking against frame

recycling nicked from bins

footsteps above

heater's hiss

City : alone is never. & silence a stranger's pause
between strike & inhale : the length from match
to tobacco : cough, cough, heels applauding asphalt.
"The Concept-city is decaying. Does that mean   [*The Practice of*
the illness affecting the rationality that founded it   *Everyday Life—*
afflicts the urban population as well?" & who is it   Michel
the city counts as subject? If this white woman   de Certeau]
buries needles beneath the front sidewalk tree in dirt
I can't dig in to plant grass I'd call by name, who do
I count? I can't qualify another subject's suffering
yet—

"at the edge   [*The Object*
of what is bearable   *Stares Back—*
in an image"   James Elkins]

she o.d.s on our stoop.

To witness is nothing if to remember her remains
a white matchbook's four corners blackened
by blood, a particular weather carried arterial :
sticky panic sweating a shirt through, fear a pulse
quickened by pity. Her image escapes meaning
differently than the city's ephemeral privacies
disquiet my own : a profile turns a corner; tortillas
fry in the flat above; a man stows his bedroll
to keep it dry; water curbs to sewer; pipes siphon,
knock—

                                old oil sours

                    the alley;

                    I look again

                                      she's gone—

Later that day at Chimney Rock we saw below the path
a cat sunning—"Is that a cat?" I asked—pricking its ears
it flew to clustered firs. Earlier we'd heard its *who who*
over the ridge, weird to hear owl & ocean both.
We were still sitting. I was making nouns simpler :
dirt   wind   cliff   stone   blue   blue   blue
blue   (each depth-dependant);

                                        I was making language
                        a stem to aspire to :

                        durable   flexible   able
                                    to register shift quickly—

                        when shaken
                                    to keep shape.

A guidebook calls it "Tall Flatsedge" but at my desk
it doesn't stick : each sketched notebook detail floats
slowly from what once had made it live. At its smallest
"matter has no ideals" : taking off my socks, I find
several flatsedge seeds hooked home : no split of self
from self—it can't lack—carbon, oxygen, nitrogen—
it's being & being singly is. All day at Chimney Rock
I'd returned to three thoughts :

[*Plants of the
San Francisco Bay
Region*—Kozloff
& Beidleman]

[*Manuscript
Lectures*—
William
James]

              you; the "world

     we wanted   to go out into,
              to come to ourselves   into";

   & the right form
              to bridge two subjects apart

                    if
   "organizations in the sound of them
              verg[e] upon meaning,
                    upon 'Heaven'"—

["Dante Études"—
     Robert Duncan]

                                        now on the stoop
a woman works into cornrows her friend's hair :
comb & fingers pull the good wool tight, exposed
scalp bright, her tin within reach : Vaseline,
barrettes, a spool of white string. Their talk echoes
easy upstairs to where we continue between us
to build a life & I endeavor here

                        stress upon stress   until

                        though in the other room you're reading

                        a bridge is where we are

                                        there's no apart

                                [*March 2007—January 2008*]

II

TRANSCENDENTAL GRAMMAR CROWN

I had no Monarch in my life, and cannot rule myself,
and when I try to organize—my little Force explodes—
—E.D. to Higginson

I gazed long. I saw how mutability and unchangeableness
were united.
—Fuller, Summer on the Lakes

But we would rather believe that music is beyond any
analogy with word language…
—Ives, Essays Before a Sonata

You cannot hear music and noise at the same time.
We avoid all the calamities that may occur in a lower
sphere by abiding perpetually in a higher.
—Thoreau, Journals

Health, south wind, books, old trees, a boat, a friend.
—Emerson, Journals

THE LEAP FROM MATTER

(*Idealism*)

abstraction   lays waste

to day   ox-eye knodding

roadside   can't help

but fail touch   if the real

must be monument   to a systemic thinking   —it's not   that we don't

cotton to optimism   just   from the local   purview   it looks like rain   :

when we're in bed   & eavesward   thunder tumbles   to shake the panes

we think about   oiling

our boots   —which is

to say   to be our body is sticky   hurt fir   white-green lichen   the fawn's

brown sides   shot through with spots   like pastured asters   we walk in

skin   & salamanders exactly   the orange of old pine   & still we love

our minds   *do* seem clearer   the way quartz tricks a window   into earth

OUR MINDS DO SEEM
(Rain Guide)

unending silver gilding   whose color   surface

doesn't suffer   like light's   clarifies outline   :

lily   bell   yellow   yarrow   vetch   white

violet   lace   crown   —what happens is

syntax   color-

less   texture

clamor   dress

—wanting nothing   for a sentence   to make

noise sense   we went   earward to wear

appearance   a noun   a page   a field

guided to wildflowers   —is lips   is hooded

is ends in spikes   purple

paired leaves   a square

stem   :   hello   hairy skullcap

HELLO

(*Ives*)

—interval   from felt

to string   a struck

ear's   the soul's seat

set ringing   —easy

        now   song   has a few rights   can break

        a law   if it likes   if our ear veers   hymnward

        it won't wear   no ribbon   to match its voice

—intellect is never

a whole   soul

finds things there

        —must a song   always

        be a song

        some

        in this book   can't be sung

THIS BOOK CAN'T BE SUNG

(*Reading Walden*)

—solitude   self-definition   :   pure

nationalism!   beans in a row   & a year

to hoe them   heroic vatic stance struck mock

epic   all ironic to trick the mind   into seeing

America   a masculine parable   a second-growth

forest   to walk there   an easy wilderness   vernacular

apples   your grammar so declarative   it *is*

a government   —prophetic voice   come

closer   bring your certitude   so we can pinch

it to pith   force it   to the far wrong side

of moribund bachelorhood   we are stunned blood

we are inherited citizen dualism   we must begin

to ring   must in your ears   rebuttal   stuffed

with spirit   your whole ruddy skin   stung with it

INHERITED CITIZEN DUALISM

(*Field Poetics*)

doubt   entered the field

in the form of a body

always   grass at edge

calf-high   then rising

as heat   midday does

waist-length

       —transcendent   reason   :   mind forsaking

matter it finds   impossible questions

              to consider   —roots

              cool   green   below

              browning stems   it

              didn't want to   eat

              our mouth   intended

              to tangle   is not

              mind   it's never

              wanted   for order

OUR MOUTH IS NOT MIND

(*E.D.*)

you will never forgive us

for we never visit   sick

with god-longing   livid

fever   reeling   bestial

need sends us on all fours   in the field   where heat

ends mid-stem   spectrum's very heaven   boils above

hawkweed & birdsfoot   trefoil & a roil   of inflorescence

—doubt   a terrible field

to live in   whose laws

are made by a god

without cause or qualities

were we to cry out   lord   our voice   the wrong season

for milkweed   it's the only thing   to come home to is

what scatters   what's always going away

WHAT'S

(—)

as saint

is slant

to pain

       storm   norm numb null

       thorn   pressed to thumb

as wait

is pain's

time's

plait

       in all's

       stall   what becomes

       of becoming

fear

nadir of feeling

OF FEELING

(*Sonnet*)

—no monument   no moment   no human

passion   just spider's fiber   cantilevered

thing   hedged   best guess   a net

to register   the transparency   identity

becomes   its minimal matter   fragile

—& then what   plaint & wait   as if

your whole life   a pattern of spectacular

aptitude   for disappointment   your

intelligence   a broken wing   a bird

feigns   to distract the hunt   from kill

—it's useless   to reduce gesture   further dear

form   :   are you reason   are you even feeling   :   fail better

FAIL BETTER

(Thoreauvian)

—solstice brings the field

to its knees   yarrow

flax   vetch   heavy

estival air a gall of pollen

—& aren't you novice   again in lit   Euclidean gilt

shadows to true   each natural fact   toward more

radical matter   :   a robe of rhetoric   auric eulalia

—to angle praise   fodder the color of how you felt

as a child   pure Bible-light   ochre smoke & ivory

vellum pages   cut stems   sweet   —taller now

than grass   you can't

but muster   nothing

longing a rope you'd use

to haul it all   other-wise

OTHER-WISE
(*Grasses Parable*)

—to have been built bent

to bear witness   to have

been thin-stemmed   spined

like a mind   to have said

—it's true   we saw the grasses   turned snake

flesh   fall crept cribs of cryptic ribs   we wished

it was a dream   but the fields   went weird & left

—was it a dream   at forest's edge   we watched

dark arc over the fields   how trees begin to lean

at that hour over   their own shadows   & the voice

called the grasses   back

by name   —timothy

bent   orchard   hair

poverty   sweet vernal   come

SWEET VERNAL

(*The Over-Soul*)

above   the canopy creaks

wood on wood   exactly

the sound   of docks

on the lakes of our childhood

& wind   :   water walking

awkwardly on top of itself   toward shore   —the problem with solitude is

each fact is twice   :   once ours once   its own   :   & so vision   is question

& response   is also twice   sight besets the trees   that are memory also

& wind   water that touched shore so long ago   it washes up here   above

—you said the soul   knows only

the soul   sight seems our own

& doesn't   why a lake sound

high in the trees   why the smell

of hay   sweeter than seeing

VISION IS QUESTION

(*Ives : July 4ᵗʰ*)

afternoon encumbered

by thunder   birches

turned dirty   curvy

piss-yellow stormlight

& someone singing   behind the trees' screen   *a place in the soul*

                                        all made of tunes   of long ago
    "a certain
                                        —but it is hard   to love
        kind of ecstasy"
                                        old men's   sentimental

                                        off-key singing   even

when beauty   moved them   as it moves us   to watch fire

works in wartime   eerie green
                                        "but they sing
mimetic   sound of missiles
                                          in my soul"
whistling   bitter smoke

smothers the field   a song our fathers loved   : *Shall we   gather at the river?*

THE FIELD A SONG

(*Leaving New England*)

in the field   we dream

west   how poppies tip

toward orange   *heliotropic*

a word yellow   edge a furl

fragrant   —to say good-bye   is specific

                 as the node where grass branches   & stem

intends   *inflorescence*   a word we love

           where it clusters   fuzz   most modest

of blossoms   green timothy sheathed

          of a sudden   in yellow   —we lie

          on our backs   a view   framed by grass

          & light rises   three times   the owl

          sounds round   as a nest   :   the very

          air crows thwart   their throats upon

THE VERY AIR
(*Faith Reason*)

but we tire   of spirit   sight

    striving always   for elsewhere as we are

so much   among phenomena   God

    loses luster   where we are local only   inured

to detail   starting small   with grasses

    flowers then trees   we don't know   nor rocks

days   to recite the names   of them all

    seems heaven enough   to us   because what is

language that   "categories of thought

    embodied in individual living forms"   thread through us

& things equally   —matter   a sidereal charity

    & doesn't it bract   doesn't it sepal & send seed splitting sheath

into soil   doesn't our flesh   the very fossils   tremble bedrock

FOSSILS TREMBLE

(*Matter Gap*)

it's easier   to walk now

through grammar   colonial stone

wall fallen   to gaps   on soft needle

plush   sprung rust rot so acid

nothing else can grow   —you would know   is it soul the fern

interrupts itself   to reproduce   it is easier   to ask now

if grammar better follows nature   to die in cycle   than culture

in ruin   the gaps are different   aren't they   —but neither

better explains   how to say

anything   where to put each word

so it lives differently   in relation

to the real   as it dies   what is it

to be   the leap from matter

to a transcendental   grammar

III

ATLAS PEAK

Dirt path; berry-black scat; grass nest—

                          the old corral's white paint

                                          whiter for summer's

       colors ending
          in the fields, weathered

                                      silver stalks.

Inside the red gate we paused, rust on our fingers; a chain held the path behind us shut. Up, past the abandoned corral, through bracken, after a felled tree forked the way, rightwards up & even steeper, lay the ridge. But we paused under a bare oak where trucks had once stuck—leaves glutted their ruts. We paused, day empty of horses. We, absent the sweetness of hay.

Rocky, uneven, enclosed by chaparral then opening onto pasture, our sightline belonged solely to path. Deer-track lent color, umber & ochre; rock, light-struck, chips of scintilla; bark, lichen's mimic signature. It was like having to choose—matter or the look of matter?—& getting lost in the distance before a choice. We walked there, seeing the way scat contains hunger's evidence & residue—seed, fiber, fur, bone. Thus concentrated, vision became more.

From the path

its fence seemed

to enclose nothing   but over it horizon

of its own   we felt

                                                  held an inverted bowl—

―――――――――――

eastward the peak

rose   to the west
   over the plateau;   the ridge crested

                       & fell

               to the valley's trough—

Left then unto meadow; unto countless contradictory crisscrossed winnowed ways across its acreage; left unto burrs & thistle slivering our shins, unto branch-slap unto scratch & sting & welt; left until upward dead-end & backtrack led us to where the tree's tilt split the earth we'd wanted to stand at edge of, to where *wander* showed us sundown held in its crown, horizon its root in air.

———————————

We paused again outside the gate. More than home I desired the sleep-colored grasses—burnishing, turning silvers. I wanted to keep inside the shut eye the look of them, inflorescence spent & toppled bent stalk, wind handling their panicles: a dream arranged down to its smallest logic: this way dark & that way shine until there's only one way back. You called my name, & the moment stayed, the only scent my face in your neck.

so the corral enclosed

                                                flattened, fanned out

something

                                                a pearlescent gray

if only it was our wish for it,

                                                where lately had slept

as our wish for the grasses—

                                                what?—

            was also its shape.

To begin with the desire
　　　to begin without a title—like

　　　　　we spend our seconds slowly
　　　deciding a trail
　　　　　to take, the slower to adore

　　more the rhetoric of a choice
& lend logos to whim's

irrepressible stretchy
　　　syntax, the poem for a time

　　　　　both kinesis & mimesis, process
　　　& scene, body & world, our
　　　　　selves doubled, stationed between two

　　possibilities continuous
rather than discrete—

first Heidegger claims
　　　poetry's words shelter

　　　　　"the poetic statement
　　　as that which by its essential
　　　　　nature remains unspoken,"

　　then Irigaray asks
"Does he bring about

both a distinction between
        these two and a confusion of them?

            How not mistake them?
    By suspending yes and no?"
            —& so without choosing

        we keep hiking, since
there's no harm going

further afield now we've left
        the cabin for a day of chill sun,

                high wind, trees, blackbirds'
            wings' red in the mock
                orange adamant as larkspur

        against darker underbrush.
    It's not far to the first gate,

just as far as anyone is
        "justified, be he [sic]

                an authority or a layman,
            in expressing or trying to
                express in terms of music

        (in sounds, if you like),"
    Ives begins *Essays Before a Sonata*,

"the value of anything
        which is usually expressed

                in terms other than music."
            Discursion & *excursion*
                share a root, *currere*, to run :

        an octave opens Ives' Sonata,
    two hands spanning a "b"

from which they both depart,
  forte & "Slowly," in opposite

    directions; the hike begins
   with two gates, one of steel
    & one wood, one closed

  & one open; between
lie the fields which are like

nothing but themselves
  except in how they change

    depending on the time
  of day & the season :
   May 21st, spring's end,

  with this deixis it's almost noon;
soon the sun, centered

directly above, will lend
  the live grasses a hard, flat aspect,

    so as we close the steel gate,
  the fields—their particular
   clarity beholden today

  to cloudless sky—seem one
seamless surface, rough,

tufted, unevenly green & gold,
  stretched from boulder

    to oak to trail, imperturbable
  furze broken only by scattered
   wildflowers. Last night I dreamt

  I slept against that tree
& a rattlesnake, biting

my wrist, curled a copper band
        up my arm. I walked back to the first gate,

                but it was locked & I wasn't sorry
        the spiky heat in my head
                gathered in sheaves of *Carex scoparia*...

        A linguistic event coextensive
with the hike itself,

the poem can't hold the real
        fields, of course—unsaid,

                implicit, "the poetic
        statement" can't say
                what it means to *be*

        in the fields, locate their value
or convey their biodiversity;

we're meant to discuss,
        "first, to point out

                the proper place or site of
        something, to situate it,
                and second, to heed that

        place or site," Heidegger
writes, as we watch hawks—

two of them—ride big winds
        buffeted first east up the ridge

                then down to us who squint
        dust & walk on, "a suggestion
                of irony in the thought

        this powerful, vague but
compelling vitality

that ever sweeps us on
    in spite of ourselves"

        (Ives writes of Emerson),
    is a good hike's trajectory,
        which, like the *Concord* Sonata's

    first movement, repeats
central themes gesturally,

through variation : to begin
    with the desire for accuracy,

        to examine the lichen
        to our right, its surprise white
        turquoise patching over

    most of the boulder,
even the branch-ends

of the adjacent dead bush,
    its interior alive with grass

        thrusting up through
      empty branches
        inflorescences fat

    broad, gold as barley,
wiry, upright, tufted

thick, the poem *transcriptive*
    rather than descriptive.

        As Duncan says, "In faith
    my sight is sound"—
        the movement ends,

    the second gate near
as noon, red & wide

& open to upward.

II.

Like the pause in the song

     of the Towhee—*tsip*
   tsip—whose weight barely
       bends the bunchgrass stem—

  a caesura : "the whole being
of the singing soul single,

concentrated," then | |
    from Latin for "cutting," but

      also in music | | a breather;
    the second movement begins
      again as a permanent artifact

   situated in time, a paradox
this time *pianissimo, subito*

hymnal, before we return to
    the scherzo—but sinister,

      like how I love the red
    gate is always open, but
      remember as we pass

   through it, in the woods
beyond lies Tucker, horse

of storied burial, horse
of unlucky afterlife :

accident left him trailside
a half-mile short of his grave,
so he was skinned, left

two weeks unburied,
then moved twenty feet

off trail & covered by too little
dirt, a grave marked by his own

exposed head. Now his pale
skull, skewed jaw mark it
still, & I always think of him

when we pass under the oak,
coolest shade of any tree :

quakinggrass grows there
green until June, a ring of it

wide as the oak's canopy :
a thought that returns
only in its shade, only after

the thought of Tucker nearby,
the way "a rare experience

of a moment at daybreak,
when something

seems to reveal all
consciousness," Ives writes,
"cannot be explained

at noon." But it *is* noon,
dust reddens our boots,

there are twenty minutes
        still to the ridge, the poem

                remains untitled; we will
                have to explain our belatedness
                all the way uphill, explicate

        our smutty cuffs, my habit
of quotation, our cotton socks

already flecked with seed
        itching our ankles & feet;

                "it is a part of the day's unity,"
                Ives would say, but we will
                have to prove it. We will

        have to make it so. We will
have to begin as our forebears

did, with the desire to sing,
        bareheaded, full of sentiment, up

                past oaks & graves & empty
                corral reclaimed by grassland,
                habitat of the brown-headed

        cowbird, whose song, says
A Guide to Western Birds, "consists of

explosive squeaking bubbling
        notes," whose song, I say,

                exceeds liquidity through many
                recessed hinges, part of the day's
                unity being Ives' assertion

        "spirit is sounded,"
& though I'm aware

reading a lyric produces
        a theory of lyric that then

                produces a reading of lyric,
            as Virginia Jackson notes,
                a "hermeneutic circle

        rarely open to dialectical
interruption," my mode is

fundamentally standing
        at the margin & letting

                things in : from the north,
            as though there thought
                opens, they enter, the field

        larger than singular, the path
veering sharply west, grass

land giving way to dense
        chaparral & manzanita,

                the enormous fragility of
            dialectics a permission
                regarding writing, "this pivot

        of a totality having no total
thing in us," Duncan writes,

"we so live beyond ourselves,"
        hike always already annotated

                by coyotes' scrupulous scat
            drying white among boulders
                splashed with birdshit, all

        a part of the path. Maybe

III.

to begin with the desire

to give thought to the site
      (as Heidegger would say),

          to language that which
        "from a metaphysical-
          aesthetic point of view

      may at first appear to be
a rhythm," is to risk authoring

context as part of the lyric
      only to fail at both, though

          Ives swears "all melodious poets
      shall be hoarse
          when the penetrating keynote

      of nature and spirit
is sounded," or maybe

virtuosity too much informs
      my ideal, a design I'd play

          the way Ives' Sonata asks,
        without time signatures,
          without regular measures,

      just notes & articulation—
slur, legato, staccato,

duration & volume
     in relation to each other—

       & "only the imagination
      of the Whole, the immediate
       percept is to be justified,"

    Duncan claims, since
to play it, it is true

we "have to renounce projecting
     in the solitary manner the horizon

      of a world as transcendence,"
    as Irigaray argues;
     we have to hold it instead

   in our heads & hands
which would seem impossible

except for how we remember
     the trail in our feet, calves,

      & thighs, our lungs' thrust
    upward; our eyes, which scan
     trailside bracken for flowers;

    & our minds, which recall
their names as best they can :

my favorite native, *Diogenes'*
    Lantern, hangs from each stem

      auric, folded triangular bowls
    whose brightness dries
     the color of saffron; tall ivory-

   colored cups top the *Mariposa*
Lilies, spotted inside like fox

glove, white, brown, yellow;
    Narrow-Leafed Mule Ear

        hunkers among low scrub,
      its hairy red stems lifting
        sallow blooms half daisy, half

   buttercup; we'd recognize
anywhere a branch of *Sticky*

Monkeyflower, which breeds
    itself out of rock & fog,

        thin & tenacious as if vine
      mated shrub & burst
        into twigs hefting dozens

   of pale orange trumpets;
Dwarf Stonecup is a struggle,

a red-fleshed succulent
    feeding on the boulders

        from which it shrugs
      flowers; *Frying Pan*
        Poppies, cousins of

   the state flower, at sunset
twist shut their pale

gradated heliotropic
    yellows; & *Bird's Eye Gilia*,

        its five white petals fringed
      pink-violet, produces blue
        pollen we have to stoop to

   see, that flower's so small.
This is my favorite thing :

when space shrinks, time
        expands : ten minutes vanish

                into one flower, less than
        one square inch of earth.
                "Rather than present a series

        of immutable frames in our
understanding of landscape,"

writes Christophe Girot,
        let's "attempt to imagine a new

                form of thinking that can
        integrate the traveling
                continuum of time and space,"

        which is why we hike
on the cusp of summer

when the flora has bloomed
        but isn't yet dead, so we see it

                seasonal, measured,
        articulated by seed
                & dispersal, the radical

        scatter of energy, green
just before dry July sun

& the risk of wildfires
        some seeds—manzanita,

                the Frying Pan Poppy—
        depend on for release,
                what Duncan would call

        "design toward crisis."
To read is like that,

& to love—
    "in reading / space

        & time / Life writing
      in each mind / teems,"
        Duncan writes, "his mind

      ours / sublime community."
For twenty feet up ahead

we'll duck under manzanita;
      when we stand again we'll see

      fifty miles to San Francisco.

IV.

      Profuse chamise,
        rose's cousin, smothers the path

    in pin-sized blossoms, petals
powdering our sleeves

white. At ridge's edge,
    lone among the rocks, violet

      Harvest Brodiaea blooms now
    the surrounding grasses
      have withered, reseeded.

    The Valley from Bay to Angwin is
visible by virtue of one tall boulder—

often I climb up
    & find myself thinking

        of my father dead now a year,
      how near I was to him
        in my ambivalence; he was

    the thing I held away
& so held it closer

for how intently I examined it
    thinking myself safe

        from influence. I loved him
      before I knew anything
        about him——the way I loved

    Heidegger, Ives, Duncan,
& the idea of California,

all four essentially crazy
    with ambition, injured,

        unethical, genius, sweetly
      suckered by beauty
        & the thought of beauty.

    So much of our seeing
lies in forgetting the laws

of the fathers, the ones
    we were given, & the ones

        we choose, as though we look
      always at landscape first
        through their eyes, a valencing

    scrim of quotation, before
we blink & see——what?

What we love, how we care for it,
    is where we live : bay trees

        so potent today after last night's rain
      our shirts smell still
        of leaves we barely brushed by; walking

    with my thumb in a book
to mark a thought; returning

to this place to revisit a feeling;
    how the Wappo populated

        Talahalusi before the Spanish
      & smallpox winnowed
        the tribe, eventually force-

marched north by U.S. military.
By mid-century, homesteaders

lived up here, white folks
    chopping wood, making charcoal,

        hauling it through rocky chaparral,
      down steep miles from the peak—
        why choose to farm impossibly

    rocky land so far from town?
Why cull stone after stone

to stack into miles of fence
    high as a tall man's waist, why

        labor on a cliff's edge
      except for money,
        beauty, hunger, manifest

    destiny, all the myths of the West,
the father as realm,

how one by one all
    the small towns of the mind

        light up? Napa, Vallejo, Carneros…
    sometimes it makes me sick,
        the valley's parti-colored grid

    rippling with rows of grapes or cash
crops, each block bordered

by asphalt, bright cars of tourists
    or migrant workers or the fertilizer

        whose nitrates are a major non-point
    source pollutant, diminishing
        wetlands shimmering in the distance.

    "Think of our life in nature,
—daily to be shown matter,

to come in contact with it—,"
    wrote Thoreau, lost on Ktaadn,

        "the *actual* world! *Who* are we? *where*
    are we?" I, Space, & you,
        Time, should marry the world

    as it is, as Wittgenstein said
it was : everything

that is the case : hawk, cirrostratus,
    chainsaw, a California that changes

        the ear to see the eye to hear
    to sing, to attend to
        the day's duties : a band of dark

    red on the leaf sheath; black
on the tip of the tail;

bright chestnut brown acorns;
    dark brown on a long tail's tip;

        deep purple cones tinged with brown;
    a grayer face; grayish, deeply
        furrowed bark; a guttural rattle;

    a height of 75 to 110 feet;
a high-pitched screaming

aack; an iridescent dark rose
    cap & throat; leafy bracts;

        linear-oblong pinnules; infolded
    margins; a purple sheen
        on the neck; a red-spotted nape;

    scaly brown flower clusters;
short, inconspicuous ear tufts;

smaller plumes; sterile leaves
    evergreen; stripes on the face;

        triangular stems; *tsit-tsoo-tsee-tsay*;
    twenty-two teeth; two short
        rising notes followed by a rapid trill;

    underground stems covered
with chestnut-colored scales;

& well-developed scent glands—
    but totality doesn't end. We do,

        bereft of breath, our senses shushed
    before we've finished
        our work, listening like the pianist

    shuts the lid on strings still vibrating :
the last chord lingers, stings those

left to hear it. It sounds like Emerson
    writing Thoreau : "Will you not come up

        to the Cliff this p.m. at any hour
        convenient to you...
            if you will, bring your flute

    for the echo's sake, though now
the wind blows." Fatherless

afternoon, very untitled death,
    my father's voice returns as echo

        of my own *good-bye*, restoring to his absence
        all lost, inaccessible inflections,
            the way a face in turning away is differently

    lit by the sight of what it's turned toward
...here the score plays out its final bars,

each hand in a different key,
    mine kinesis & yours mimesis,

        one the body & the other the world,
        the song doubled, stationed
            between two consonances continuous

    rather than discrete, the resultant music
dissonant not because of distance

but because of our proximity
    to each other, the final chord

        followed by a fermata over the final
        barline, a silence endless
            as the air into which our fathers

    last looked out, thinking, like Thoreau,
"Here was no man's garden,

but the unhandselled globe.
     It was not lawn, nor pasture

          nor mead, nor woodland, nor lea
          nor arable, nor wasteland.
          It was Matter, vast, terrific…

     the felt presence of a force not bound
to be kind to man." It's how

our fathers' rest ends in us :
     we stand & start toward the angle

          the afternoon light leans against
          the long stone wall
               farther up the ridge : it's there

     the path ascends to Atlas Peak
where we'll bury their vision in air—

Robert J. Teare
February 9, 1933—June 13, 2007

[Atlas Peak, May 20—27, 2008]

STAR THISTLE

(*Centaurea solstitialis*)

He died & lamplight
that night brought out against fog its grid of gambits,

each street a perfect winter
dissembled : pure effect,

after that, anything outside
all scumble : marine layer a low hover

that suffered dwelling to disappear into weather, façade
a slow fade into gradient :

his death felt like that :
to unlock & open the front door onto a lost element

looking for purchase, to find a vanishing inside
a home where once there'd been rooms

& no humus
into which to inter his memory, no image :

from fifty miles away, a thousand feet below the field I love,
I tried to remember

how spring undoes the year like a knot :
how winter hay's flat thin cover turns gold,

gray beneath rain, keeps close to ground
the germinal heat :

how grasses thread up through
the remainder of what sowed them

& help break it down : all spring following his death
I turned in thought to pale green

stems infiltrating the annual
weave of leavings, each seed a knot in the energy net

flung out over the field
so the caught space can blossom :

June 4th I board the ferry in time to see spring end
on Atlas Peak, grasses turning again to seed :

each stem an eidolon of itself, brittle
inflorescences shattering

in my wake, I leave the cabin
each afternoon for the field's edge

to sit & watch what I can't see
work the surface : wind, which I've never cared for

in particular, cares *only* for
particulars : this rachis, this spikelet, these lodicules,

nothing too miniature to be seized by a shaking
neither grief nor fear

& far more complete :
days I close my eyes I hear the smallest ocean's smallest surf break

beneath my feet a pile of gold seeds that rattles the dust :
after fourteen years of living with HIV & the side effects of protease inhibitors,

after persistent, misdiagnosed abdominal pain
turned out to be colon cancer that'd spread to his liver,

after the removal of the tumor & the majority of his colon,
after chemotherapy's nausea & neuropathy,

after "a perforated abdomen led to a heart attack"
following "three surgeries, and a seizure after the second surgery,"

after "severe peritonitis
and a very bad case of blood poisoning"

that almost killed him,
Reginald died, his final letter

to me ending as always,
"Take good care my friend" : a gesture

I leave the field to hike up the trail
thick with wildflowers : less vetch this year, but plenty of mariposa lilies,

all the flowers bountiful until halfway to the ridge
I enter another field

of a liminal tint, blue-green
stems covered in pale hair, thousands still tender,

but others older, each branch ending in a bright ball of spikes
soon to bloom : yellow star thistle,

non-native invasive,
particularly noxious to grazing animals :

each year the thistle spreads farther down trail :
each year each plant bears

one to a thousand seed heads,
each seed head holding as many as eighty seeds, the life of one plant

easily leaving one hundred behind : knowing nothing I do will help
I pull up a hundred young plants

each time I pass the first field of them :
I grip each stem low to ensure I get

the long ingenious taproot
that even during drought reaches water

& my forearms blister where they're pricked by lateral spines :
it might be bad mourning

to want the thistle gone
but I go on hating it :

it seems an uncanny design
ensures its slow destruction of an ecosystem :

it chokes out healthy grassland flora, even kills grazing animals
that might control its spread :

uncanny it survives drought & thrives
off wildfire both :

just a pretty plant holistic in its grip of a habitat,
the thistle is not metaphor

& extends into the future
as far as I can see, easily filling the field I love :

at its edge I stand, my skin
a stipple of blisters :

Something startles me where I thought I was safest...
Whitman says,

Now I am terrified
at the Earth, it is that calm and patient

as it undoes itself, undoing that toughens
to give way relentlessly to nothing

but its own propagation : the Earth
undoes itself as each life undoes itself & to what end

is what terrifies me as after the hike
I try with salve to soothe the blisters that deepen & weep weird clear fluid :

the day before Reginald died, we spoke on the phone
but morphine filled his speech

so completely
it was terrible to listen to him, disappearing

even as he said I love you & I echoed him, the last thing
I could bear

before I had to say goodbye
filled with the certainty I'd failed to witness the death of a friend I'd loved :

good mourning accepts transience, sure :
it makes sense in the field I love

where I see next year already
on the stem : sun draws inflorescences taut

& wind separates what's left into seed & chaff : but
I was raised to believe in

a personal God attending a death
whose final horizon is eternity, an ideal persistent

as the star thistle seeds carried to California by contaminated feed in the 1850s,
whose progeny covers twelve to fifteen million acres currently :

what chemistry!
as Whitman would say

it is that calm and patient :
& though the thistle isn't metaphor

I find myself kneeling,
weeding the lowest field again, & I become everything

about root giving up ground, the groan it grudges as it eases up, out,
the subtle scent of the flower

that when eaten by horses causes brain lesions
& mucosal mouth ulcers that lead to eventual death by starvation & dehydration

& when eaten by bees makes exceptional honey, heavily fragrant
& strangely dark, almost grey :

two weeks before we spoke, Reginald in the hospital wrote his last poem,
"God-With-Us," ending it

...How I want
to believe. (a pearl, an irritant). :

it's one thing to want to believe, to live by building a mind on the fault
between faith & doubt :

it's another to believe the longing for belief
an attack, a distrust of immersion in the material given us as habit & habitat,

no possible rush of friendship for stones, grasses & humus,
as if the human were over

& the wild deer in us were released at last
at dusk to disappear into the stand of manzanita far across the field I love :

if we die to become nothing but matter so that Being itself might continue,
grounded by ground itself,

such a sweet thing out of such corruptions!,
who wouldn't wish to linger in the material world

that won't spare me or let me hold a living hand to him :
all spring I'll return

to bring grief to the field, always
one root

I can't pull out
entire : "as above,

so below" :
from star down to thistle

it's all the same : still firm in the ground,
today it breaks in my hand,

bad mourning that this summer flowers
the life only destruction makes possible.

Reginald Shepherd
April 10, 1963 — September 10, 2008

ACKNOWLEDGEMENTS

:: Many thanks to the editors of the following journals and websites in which versions of these poems appeared:

> *Boston Review*: "The very air" & "Fossils tremble"
> *The Chronicle of Higher Education* blog: "Hello"
> *Colorado Review*: "Little Errand"
> *Denver Quarterly*: "Quakinggrass" & "Atlas Peak"
> *Hotel Amerika*: "Tall Flatsedge Notebook"
> *New England Review*: "Star Thistle"
> */nor*: "Sussurrus Stanzas"
> *Pleiades*: "White Graphite"
> *Poetry Daily*: "The very air" & "Fossils tremble"
> *The Rumpus*: "Largo"
> *Seattle Review*: "To begin with the desire"
> *VOLT*: "Vision is question"

:: I also owe thanks to the editors and publishers of the following chapbooks and anthologies, folks who so graciously shepherded the work into the world and folks who also reprinted it:

> "Atlas Peak" was commissioned by Michael Montlack as a tribute to Virginia Woolf, and was reprinted in *Divining Divas: 100 Gay Men on Their Muses*, which was edited by Michael & published by Lethe Press in 2012.

> "Largo" was reprinted in the *The Rumpus Original Anthology of Contemporary Poetry*, published by The Rumpus in 2012. Thanks to Brian Spears and Andrew Altschul for the support.

> "To begin with the desire" won the 2009 Pavement Saw Press chapbook competition and was first published in 2011 under the title of ↑. Many thanks to editor and publisher David Baratier for choosing the poem and shepherding it so carefully into publication.

"Transcendental Grammar Crown" was first published as a chapbook by Woodland Editions in 2006. Many thanks to Jaime Robles, Susanne Dyckman and Todd Melicker for asking for work and publishing it so beautifully.

"This book can't be sung," "Inherited citizen dualism," "Our mouth is not mind," and "What's" from "Transcendental Grammar Crown" also appeared in *Joyful Noise: An Anthology of American Spiritual Poetry*, edited by Robert Strong and published by Autumn House in 2006.

"Transcendental Grammar Crown" in its entirety also appeared in *The Arcadia Project: North American Postmodern Pastoral*, edited by Joshua Corey and G.C. Waldrep and published by Ahsahta Press in 2012.

:: Thank you ::

To the administrators who gave me work in the Bay Area during the years when I was writing this book—Kate Brady and Aaron Shurin at the University of San Francisco, Joseph Lease and Ann Joslin Williams at the California College of the Arts, Edie Meidav and Sarah Stone at the New College of California, and Cynthia Scheinberg and Juliana Spahr at Mills College—I remain grateful. To the dedicated students I worked with at each of these institutions, I am indebted.

"Transcendental Grammar Crown" couldn't have been written without the support of the MacDowell Colony in 2005. The composition of the poem and much of the book that followed greatly benefited from a copy of *The Essays of Henry David Thoreau* that was gifted to me while I was in residence—thank you, Lewis Hyde.

The entirety of the book's third section couldn't have been written without the support of Jane Mead, who graciously gave me time & space to write on Atlas Peak.

The book wouldn't exist without the love, patience, and support of Robert Barber, who gave me a home.

:: And finally, many friends and colleagues—through conversation and close reading and by the example of their work—supported the writing and editing of this book over many years:

George Albon, Rick Barot, Dan Beachy-Quick, Rachel Berchten, Gillian Conoley, Joshua Corey, Susanne Dyckman, Lisa Fishman, Kathleen Fraser, Richard Greenfield, Kate Greenstreet, Sarah Gridley, Brenda Hillman, Janet Holmes, Sally Keith, Melissa Kwasny, Jane Mead, Todd Melicker, Catherine Meng, Rachel Moritz, Rusty Morrison, Stephen Motika, Nathanaël, Peter O'Leary, G. E. Patterson, Juliet Patterson, Frances Richard, Elizabeth Robinson, Jaime Robles, Margaret Ronda, Martha Ronk, Rob Schlegel, Reginald Shepherd, Aaron Shurin, Jonathan Skinner, Michael Snediker, Carol Snow, Lisa Russ Spaar, Juliana Spahr, Jared Stanley, Robert Strong, Catherine Taylor, Jean Valentine, G. C. Waldrep, Laura Walker, Kerri Webster, Joshua Weiner and Andrew Zawacki.

NOTES

Given that the poems in *Companion Grasses* actively practice what Jed Rasula in *This Compost: Ecological Imperatives in American Poetry* calls "wreading"—a "nosing into the compost library"—what follows is largely bibliographic information about the texts that composed the "ecology of mind" from which the poems emerged. Given their composted states, the referenced texts might persist into the poems as either quoted or appropriated passages; whatever traces remain serve as evidence of an active engagement with the originals, which in all cases were inspirational in the sense that they helped the poems to breathe.

Epigraph

Blaser, Robin. "the sounding air." *Pell Mell.* Toronto: Coach House Press, 1988.

I

White Graphite

Wilson, Emily. "Nonesuch." *The Keep.* Iowa City: University of Iowa Press, 2001.

Sussurrus Stanzas

Fuller, Margaret. *Summer on the Lakes, During 1843. The Portable Margaret Fuller.* Ed. Mary Kelley. New York: Penguin Books, 1994.

Harrison, Robert Pogue. *The Dominion of the Dead.* Chicago: University of Chicago Press, 2005.

Hillman, Brenda. "Songless Era." *Cascadia.* Middletown: Wesleyan University Press, 2001.

Johnson, Ronald. *ARK.* Albuquerque: Living Batch Press, 1996.

Merleau-Ponty, Maurice. *The Visible and the Invisible.* Trans. Alphonso Lingis. Chicago: Northwestern University Press, 1969.

Moore, Marianne. "A Grave." *The Complete Poems of Marianne Moore.* New York: MacMillan, 1967.

Quakinggrass

This poem is for Matthew Groshek.

Barthes, Roland. *Camera Lucida.* Trans. Richard Howard. New York: Hill & Wang, 1982.

Farrand, Jr., John. *An Audubon Handbook: Western Birds.* New York: McGraw-Hill Book Company, 1988.

Largo

This poem is for Robert Barber.

Tall Flatsedge Notebook

Beidleman, Linda H. and Eugene N. Kozloff, *Plants of the San Francisco Bay Region: Mendocino to Monterey*. Berkeley: University of California Press, 2003.

de Certeau, Michel. *The Practice of Everyday Life*. Trans. Steven Rendell. Berkeley: University of California Press, 1988.

Duncan, Robert. "Dante Études." *Ground Work: Before the War*. New York: New Directions, 1984.

Elkins, James. *The Object Stares Back: On the Nature of Seeing*. New York: Harcourt, Inc., 1996.

Irigaray, Luce. *The Way of Love*. Trans. Heidi Bostic and Stephen Pluháček. New York: Continuum, 2002.

Lage, Jessica. *Point Reyes: The Complete Guide to the National Seashore and Surrounding Area*. Berkeley: Wilderness Press, 2004.

Merleau-Ponty, Maurice. *The Visible and the Invisible*. Trans. by Alphonso Lingis. Chicago: Northwestern University Press, 1969.

Richardson, Robert D. *William James: In the Maelstrom of American Modernism*. New York: Houghton Mifflin, 2006.

II

Transcendental Grammar Crown

Brown, Lauren. *Grasses: An Identification Guide*. New York: Houghton Mifflin, 1979.

Cowell, Henry and Sidney. *Charles Ives and His Music*. Oxford: Oxford University Press, 1969.

Dickinson, Emily. *Selected Letters*. Ed. Thomas H. Johnson. Cambridge: Harvard University Press, 1971.

_____. *Poems*. Ed. Brenda Hillman. Boston: Shambhala Publications, 1995.

Emerson, Ralph Waldo. *Emerson in His Journals*. Ed. Joel Porte. Cambridge: Harvard University Press, 1982.

_____. *Selections from Ralph Waldo Emerson*. Ed. Stephen E. Whicher. Boston: Houghton Mifflin, 1957.

Fuller, Margaret. *Summer on the Lakes, During 1843*. The Portable Margaret Fuller. Ed. Mary Kelley. New York: Penguin Books, 1994.

Hillman, Brenda. "A Geology." *Cascadia*. Middletown: Wesleyan University Press, 2001.

_____. "String Theory Sutra." *Pieces of Air in the Epic*. Middletown: Wesleyan University Press, 2005.

Howe, Susan. *My Emily Dickinson*. Berkeley: North Atlantic Books, 1985.

_____. "Thorow." *Singularities*. Hanover: Wesleyan University Press, 1980.

Ives, Charles. *114 Songs*. New York: Associated Music Publishers, 1975.

_____. "Postface to *114 Songs*." *Essays Before a Sonata*. Ed. Howard Boatwright. New York: W. W. Norton 1964.

_____. *Songs*. Perf. Susan Graham. Teldec, 2004.

Levin, Phillis, ed. *The Penguin Book of the Sonnet: 500 Years of the Tradition in English.* New York: Penguin Books, 2001.

Menand, Louis. *The Metaphysical Club: A Story of Ideas in America.* New York: Farrar, Straus & Giroux, 2001.

Peterson, Roger Tory and Margaret McKenny. *A Field Guide to Wildflowers of Northeastern and North-central North America.* Boston: Houghton Mifflin, 1968.

Sewall, Richard B. *The Life of Emily Dickinson.* Cambridge: Harvard University Press, 1974.

Swafford, Jan. *Charles Ives: A Life in Music.* New York: W.W. Norton, 1998.

Thoreau, Henry David. *The Journal of Henry David Thoreau.* Ed. Bradford Torrey and Francis H. Allen. New York: Dover Publications, 1962.

_____. *Walden. The Works of Thoreau.* Ed. Henry S. Canby. Boston: Houghton Mifflin, 1937.

III

Atlas Peak

Bashō, Matsuo. *The Narrow Road to the Interior and Other Writings.* Trans. Sam Hamill. Boston: Shambhala Publications, 1998.

Phillips, Carl. "The Trees." *From the Devotions.* Saint Paul: Graywolf Press, 1998.

Woolf, Virginia. *The Diary of Virginia Woolf, Volume Four: 1931-1935.* Ed. Anne Oliver Bell and Andrew McNeillie. New York: Harcourt Brace & Company, 1982.

To begin with the desire

Ammons, A.R. "The Ridge Farm." *Sumerian Vistas.* New York: W.W. Norton, 1987.

Block, Geoffrey. *Ives: Concord Sonata.* Cambridge: Cambridge University Press, 1996.

Brown, Lauren. *Grasses: An Identification Guide.* New York: Houghton Mifflin, 1979.

Burt, William H. and Richard P. Grossenheider. *A Field Guide to the Mammals.* Boston: Houghton Mifflin, 1964.

The Concord Museum, http://www.concordmuseum.org.

Conoley, Gillian. "Fatherless Afternoon." *Profane Halo.* Amherst: Verse Press, 2005.

Crampton, Beecher. *Grasses in California.* Berkeley: University of California Press, 1974.

Duncan, Robert. *Ground Work: Before the War.* New York: New Directions, 1984.

Fishman, Lisa. "Midsummer." *The Happiness Experiment.* Boise: Ahsahta Press, 2007.

Fresonke, Kris. *West of Emerson: The Design of Manifest Destiny.* Berkeley: University of California Press, 2003.

Gilbert, Roger. *Walks in the World: Representation and Experience in Modern American Poetry.* Princeton: Princeton University Press, 1981.

Girot, Christophe. "Vision in Motion: Representing Landscape in Time." *The Landscape Urbanism Reader.* Ed. Charles Waldheim. New York: Princeton Architectural Press, 2006.

Grillos, Steve J. *Ferns and Fern Allies of California.* Berkeley: University of California Press, 1966.

Harrison, Robert Pogue. *The Dominion of the Dead.* Chicago: University of Chicago Press, 2003.

Heidegger, Martin. "Language in the Poem." *On the Way to Language.* New York: Harper and Row, 1971.

Hoover, Paul. "Conjure." *Winter (Mirror).* Chicago: Flood Editions, 2002.

Irigaray, Luce. *The Forgetting of Air in Martin Heidegger*. Austin: University of Texas Press, 1999.

_____. *Sharing the World*. London: Continuum, 2008.

Ives, Charles. *Essays Before a Sonata*. Ed. Howard Boatwright. New York: W.W. Norton 1964.

_____, *Piano Sonata No. 2: Concord, Mass., 1840-1860*. Perf. Manfred Reinelt. Berlin Classics, 1998.

Jackson, Virginia. *Dickinson's Misery: A Theory of Lyric Reading*. Princeton: Princeton University Press, 2005.

Lyons, Richards & Jake Rugyt. *100 Napa County Roadside Wildflowers*. Napa: Stonecrest Press, 1996.

Niedecker, Lorine. "Wintergreen Ridge." *The Granite Pail: The Selected Poems of Lorine Niedecker*. Ed. Cid Corman. San Francisco: North Point Press, 1985.

Niehaus, Theodore & Charles L. Ripper. *A Field Guide to Pacific States Wildflowers*. Boston: Houghton Mifflin, 1976.

Rich, Adrienne. "Transcendental Etude." *The Dream of a Common Language: Poems 1974-1977*. New York: W.W. Norton, & Company, 1978.

Robinson, Jeffrey C. *The Walk: Notes on a Romantic Image*. Rochester: Dalkey Archive Press, 2006.

Solnit, Rebecca. *Savage Dreams: A Journey into the Landscape Wars of the American West*. Berkeley: University of California Press, 1999.

_____. *River of Shadows: Eadweard Muybridge and the Technological Wild West*. New York: Penguin Books, 2003.

Sudworth, George B. *Forest Trees of the Pacific Slope*. New York: Dover Publications, 1967.

Suscol Intertribal Council. http://suscol.nativeweb.org/nativeHistory.php.

Thoreau, Henry David. "Ktaadn." *The Essays of Henry David Thoreau*. Ed. Lewis Hyde. New York: North Point Press, 2002.

Star Thistle

"Centaurea genus." *EncycloWeedia*. http://www.cdfa.ca.gov/plant/ipc/weedinfo/centaurea2.htm

Phillips, Adam. *Darwin's Worms: On Life Stories and Death Stories*. New York: Basic Books, 2000.

Rasula, Jed. *This Compost: Ecological Imperatives in American Poetry*. Athens: University of Georgia Press, 2002.

Shepherd, Reginald. "A Plague for Kit Marlowe." *Angel, Interrupted*. Pittsburgh: University of Pittsburgh Press, 1996.

_____. "God-With-Us." *Red Clay Weather*. Pittsburgh: University of Pittsburgh Press, 2011.

Shumaker, Wayne. *The Occult Sciences in the Renaissance: A Study in Intellectual Patterns*. Berkeley: University of California Press, 1972.

Whitman, Walt. "This Compost." *Complete Poetry and Collected Prose*. Ed. Justin Kaplan. New York: Library of America, 1982.

A 2020 Guggenheim Fellow, Brian Teare is the author of six critically acclaimed books, including *Companion Grasses,* a finalist for the Kingsley Tufts Award, and *The Empty Form Goes All the Way to Heaven.* His most recent book, *Doomstead Days,* was longlisted for the 2019 National Book Award and a finalist for the National Book Critics Circle, Kingsley Tufts, and Lambda Literary Awards. His honors include the Four Quartets Prize, Lambda Literary and Publishing Triangle Awards, and fellowships from the NEA, the Pew Foundation, the American Antiquarian Society, the Headlands Center for the Arts, the Vermont Studio Center, and the MacDowell Colony. After over a decade of teaching and writing in the San Francisco Bay Area, and eight years in Philadelphia, he's now an Associate Professor at the University of Virginia, and lives in Charlottesville, where he makes books by hand for his micropress, Albion Books. He maintains a web presence at www.brianteare.net.

Companion Grasses
by Brian Teare

Cover and Interior text set in Perpetua Std

Cover Art:
Ives, Charles. Piano Sonata No. 2, "Concord, Mass., 1840-60."
New York: Knickerbocker Press, 1921.
&
Photographs taken by Brian Teare at Chimney Rock,
Point Reyes National Seashore, July 2012.

Cover and interior design by Cassandra Smith

Printed in the United States
by Books International, Dulles, Virginia
On 55# Glatfelter B19 Antique
Acid Free Archival Quality Recycled Paper

Omnidawn Publishing
Richmond, California
2013

Ken Keegan & Rusty Morrison, Co-Publishers & Senior Editors
Cassandra Smith, Poetry Editor & Book Designer
Gillian Hamel, Poetry Editor & OmniVerse Managing Editor
Sara Mumolo, Poetry Editor
Peter Burghardt, Poetry Editor & Book Designer
Turner Canty, Poetry Editor
Juliana Paslay, Fiction Editor & Bookstore Outreach Manager
Liza Flum, Poetry Editor & Social Media
Sharon Osmond, Poetry Editor & Bookstore Outreach
Gail Aronson, Fiction Editor
RJ Ingram, Social Media
Craig Santos Perez, Media Consultant